DERRICK ROSE

BY PAUL HOBLIN

Published by ABDO Publishing Company, PO Box 398166, Minneapolis, MN 55439. Copyright © 2012 by Abdo Consulting Group, Inc. International copyrights reserved in all countries. No part of this book may be reproduced in any form without written permission from the publisher. SportsZone™ is a trademark and logo of ABDO Publishing Company.

Printed in the United States of America,
North Mankato, Minnesota
092011
012012

 THIS BOOK CONTAINS AT LEAST 10% RECYCLED MATERIALS.

Editor: Chrös McDougall
Copy Editor: Anna Comstock
Series Design: Craig Hinton
Cover and Interior Production: Kazuko Collins

Photo Credits: Nam Y. Huh/AP Images, cover, 1, 29; Jim Prisching/AP Images, 4; M. Spencer Green/AP Images, 7, 21; Charles Rex Arbogast/AP Images, 9; Brian Kersey/AP Images, 11; Eric Gay/AP Images, 12, 24; Lance Murphey/AP Images, 15; Rich Clarkson/ NCAA Photos/AP Images, 17; Julie Jacobson/AP Images, 18; Winslow Townson/AP Images, 23; Mark J. Terrill/AP Images, 27

Library of Congress Cataloging-in-Publication Data
Hoblin, Paul.
  Derrick Rose : NBA's youngest MVP / by Paul Hoblin.
     p. cm. — (Playmakers)
  Includes bibliographical references and index.
  ISBN 978-1-61783-296-3
  1. Rose, Derrick. 2. Basketball players—United States—Biography—Juvenile literature.
I. Title.
  GV884.R619H63 2012
  796.323092—dc23
  [B]
                            2011036493

TABLE OF CONTENTS

Derrick Rose

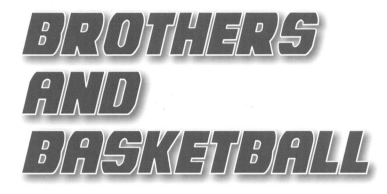

CHAPTER 1

BROTHERS AND BASKETBALL

s a kid, Derrick Rose loved to watch National Basketball Association (NBA) games on TV. He usually watched with his three brothers. They grew up in Chicago, Illinois. So, their favorite team was the Chicago Bulls.

Dwayne was Derrick's oldest brother. That meant he was in charge of the remote control. But Dwayne got nervous during close games. He sometimes had to turn off the TV!

Derrick Rose was a fan of the Chicago Bulls long before he played for them.

Derrick hated not getting to see the game. He would scream at his brother to turn the TV back on. But then he realized it was better to calm down and listen out his window. Most of the people in his neighborhood would be watching the game too. If the Bulls made a good play, they would cheer.

Derrick stayed quiet so he could hear if the Bulls were playing well. Even today, Derrick is known for being pretty quiet. Maybe that is because he learned to keep his voice down when he was a kid! Plus, Derrick could not stay mad at his brothers.

Derrick's neighborhood was not always the best place to grow up. There was lots of crime and violence there. Derrick's mom worried about him. She told his brothers to keep him safe at all times. Derrick's brothers were often very busy. But they took turns watching out for Derrick.

Derrick loves candy, especially gummi bears. He loves candy so much that his grandmother called him "Pooh." Like Derrick, Winnie the Pooh loves anything sweet. To this day, some of Derrick's teammates call him Pooh.

Derrick, his brothers Reggie, *left*, and Dwayne, *right*, and his mom pose with his 2009 NBA Rookie of the Year Award.

The older Derrick got, the more he needed his brothers' help. That is because Derrick was really good at basketball. In fact, he could dunk by the time he was in seventh grade.

There were some bad things about being so good at basketball. For one, it meant many people wanted to talk to Derrick. Sometimes, *too many* people wanted to spend time with him. Fans and reporters often followed him around wherever

By the time Derrick was in middle school, his three older brothers had full-time jobs. Dwayne did shipping and handling. Reggie was a machine operator for Pepsi. And Allan delivered computers.

he went. College recruiters did too. Derrick had not even played varsity basketball yet. Still, people would wait outside his house so they could ask him questions about his future.

One time, people learned his phone number. In one day he got nearly 40 text messages and 60 calls from total strangers.

Derrick's brothers had a plan. They said anybody wanting to talk to Derrick would have to talk to them first. That was not all they did, though. Derrick's brothers picked him up and dropped him off at school. They attended his basketball games and practices. They even did some of his shopping for him. They were doing their best to allow Derrick to be a normal kid. His favorite things to do during his free time were to go bowling or to the movie theater.

All the hype about Derrick made sense. He was already very good. He was more than 6 feet tall in middle school. Plus, he was fast, strong, and a great jumper. Derrick was also tough.

SIMEON CAREER

Derrick attended Simeon Career Academy on the South Side of Chicago.

He once hurt his right hand. So he played an entire game using only his left hand. This is hard for any player. But this was even more amazing because Derrick is right-handed.

Finally, Derrick was old enough to start high school. He went to a school in Chicago called Simeon Career Academy. Derrick led his freshman team to a city championship. He played so well that the varsity coach asked him if he wanted to play in the state championship. Derrick said no. He did not want

Derrick wore No. 25 in high school. That was the same number as Ben Wilson. He was another famous high school basketball player from Simeon Career Academy in Chicago.

to take away playing time from the varsity players who were already on the team.

The next year, Derrick did play on the varsity team. And he played very well. At the end of the season he was named a third-team All-American. And he was only a sophomore.

During his junior year, Derrick led his team all the way to a state championship. The final game was against Richwoods High School. It went into overtime. With only a few seconds to go, Derrick stole the ball from a Richwoods player. Derrick then dribbled down the court and made the game-winning shot.

Derrick was not yet done. He again led his team to the state championship as a senior. He had been a great scorer all season. But Derrick was the team's point guard. That meant his job was to do whatever it took to win the game. Sometimes that meant passing to his teammates so they could shoot instead of him. That is what he did in the state championship

Derrick led Simeon Career Academy to Illinois state championships in 2006 and 2007.

game. Derrick only scored two points. Yet he was still the star player. He finished with eight assists and seven rebounds in the 77–54 win.

Many experts felt Derrick was one of the best high school players in the United States. They were excited to see where he would play college basketball.

Derrick Rose

CHAPTER 2

COLLEGE EXPERIENCE

Deciding on a college was not easy for Derrick Rose. A lot of coaches wanted him to play basketball at their schools. But he finally decided to go to the University of Memphis in Tennessee. He announced his decision at a press conference. It was filled with reporters and fans.

Rose invited two of his teammates to the press conference. They were going to play basketball in college too. But they were not as famous as Rose.

Memphis star Rose rises above his opponent for a shot during the 2008 Final Four.

He knew that basketball is a team game. So, he felt they should get to experience the excitement of a press conference too.

Memphis was a long way from Chicago. Rose had to talk to his brothers before going there. His brother Reggie decided to go to Memphis too. That way, Rose could live with Reggie, his wife, and his daughters. Rose was glad they went. One of his favorite things to do in college was hang out with his two nieces. It made him feel like he was back home in Chicago with his family.

Rose would eventually think of his college teammates and coaches as his family too. But it took a while for him to feel comfortable around them. Rose had always been quiet. This confused some of his teammates. They did not know why he rarely talked. Even when he did say something, he often mumbled.

His teammates did know that Rose wanted to help them win games. John Calipari was the head coach at Memphis. He decided he wanted Rose on his team when he saw Rose crying after losing a game. Rose brought that same passion to Memphis.

Rose drives to the basket during a college game. He averaged 14.9 points and 4.7 assists per game as a freshman.

Rose and Calipari sometimes disagreed. The coach wanted Rose to use his natural talents more. But Rose resisted. He was afraid he would look like a show off or a ball hog. But that all changed when Memphis lost a game to Tennessee. The one thing Rose hated more than hogging the ball was losing. After that loss, Rose decided to be the best player on the court. His teammates were glad he did.

Rose led Memphis to the national championship tournament. Sixty-five of the top college basketball teams competed in the tournament. Rose scored more than 20 points per game in the tournament. He also averaged more than six rebounds and six assists per game.

Memphis won its first three games. Rose and his Memphis teammates then faced Texas. Texas had a star point guard named D. J. Augustin. Rose played great defense against him. He also played great offense. Rose scored 21 points and had nine assists. Memphis won. That meant the Tigers moved on to the Final Four.

Memphis played the UCLA Bruins next. The Bruins also had a great point guard. His name was Darren Collison. Like Rose, Collison was really fast. But once again, Rose was up to the challenge. He led his team to victory. With that, Memphis was on to the national championship game!

Rose posts up against UCLA during the 2008 Final Four. He led
Memphis to the championship game against Kansas.

Memphis played the Kansas Jayhawks in the finals. It was an exciting game. The teams were tied after 40 minutes of play. So the game went into overtime. Kansas ended up winning the game. Coach Calipari once again had to watch his star point guard cry. Rose had missed a free throw that would have won the game. But he had still had a great season. And after only one year in college, Rose was ready for the NBA.

CHAPTER 3

ROOKIE SUCCESS

Life on the basketball court had gone well for Derrick Rose. He won two state championships in high school. Then, he almost won a national title during his only year in college. But maybe his best moment yet came after that. The Chicago Bulls selected Rose with the first pick in the 2008 NBA Draft. He was going home!

Rose was also going to make a lot of money. He had been poor growing up. Now he could spend

NBA Commissioner David Stern congratulates Rose at the 2008 NBA Draft.

his money on whatever he wanted. The first thing a lot of NBA players do is buy a mansion. But not Rose. He did not want a big house. Instead, he bought a house for his mother.

Vinny Del Negro was the Bulls' head coach. He was really helpful to Rose. After every game, Del Negro gave Rose a list of questions. Some of these questions were *What worked well? What didn't? What did you learn?* Answering those questions helped Rose become a better NBA player.

Rose also had to deal with high expectations. He had a lot of family and friends in Chicago. They had watched him dominate since middle school. Now they would be able to watch him every night. Playing in Chicago also meant comparisons to Michael Jordan. Many consider the former Bulls star to be the best basketball player ever. He led the Bulls to six NBA titles during the 1990s. The pressure must have been

President Barack Obama is also from Chicago. Like Rose, he was pleased that Rose got to play for their hometown Bulls. "Derrick Rose is the man," the president once said.

It did not take long for Rose to establish himself as a star player in the NBA.

terrible. But Rose said he did not mind it. He liked the pressure because it made him want to do well.

And he did really well. Rose scored at least 10 points in his first 10 games. He was the first Bulls rookie to do that since Jordan. The NBA holds a Skills Challenge during the All-Star break. It tests players on dribbling, passing, and other skills. Rose competed in the Skills Challenge. And he won!

"They never stopped talking," Rose said about the Celtics. Rose had never liked talking very much. But to be a leader, he realized, "I've got to do it."

Rose was not finished winning things either. His Bulls won 12 of their last 16 games that season. That meant they made the playoffs. The Bulls faced the Boston Celtics in the first round. Boston had won the NBA championship the previous year. Rose and the Bulls won three games against the Celtics. However, the Celtics won the series. Even in the loss, Rose learned a good lesson. The Celtics' players spent most of every game talking to each other. To be great like them, Rose knew he would have to speak up more.

At the end of the season, Rose won something else—the NBA Rookie of the Year Award. It was a sign of bigger awards soon to come.

Rose and the Bulls put up a fight but could not get past the Boston Celtics in the 2009 NBA playoffs.

24   *Derrick Rose*

BECOMING THE BEST

errick Rose became a better leader and player during his second NBA season. He was even selected to the All-Star Game. That made Rose the Bulls' first All-Star in 12 years. He also led the Bulls to the playoffs for the second season in a row.

Rose had become one of the best point guards in the NBA. Point guards need to be good passers. They help create scoring opportunities for their

Rose goes for a layup as a member of the Eastern Conference All-Star team in 2010.

teammates. Rose was a great passer. He also was a top scorer. He even scored 39 points in one late-season win against the Boston Celtics.

Rose had a good regular season. He knew he still could get better, though. The Bulls had the same record as the year before. They had 41 wins and 41 losses. It was good enough to make the playoffs. Still, the Bulls lost in the first round. It was not good enough for Rose. He wanted to win a lot more games.

Rose worked hard on his jump shot that summer. He also got to play with some of the best players in the world. The World Championship was that summer, in 2010. That is the second biggest tournament for national basketball teams outside of the Olympic Games. Rose was one of many top young NBA players selected to play for Team USA. The team also had a few key veterans to help lead them.

The tournament was in Turkey. Team USA's final game was against the Turkish team. The Turkish fans booed every time a US player touched the ball. But Rose and his teammates kept calm. They found a way to win the World Championship. The win gave Rose a lot of confidence. The Turkish players were not

Kevin Durant, *left*, congratulates Rose during the 2010 World Championship. They led Team USA to the title.

his only competition that summer, though. Like every summer, Rose also played a lot of basketball against his three brothers. Rose had developed into an NBA star. But his brothers were still there to help him with his game.

Rose entered his third NBA season on a mission. He wanted to make the Bulls one of the best teams in the league. And he felt he was ready to lead them there.

That is exactly what he did. The Bulls won a lot of games. Their fans packed the arena to watch them play. They especially loved to watch Rose play. His crossover dribble was so good that players would trip over their own feet trying to guard him. His jump shot had gotten much better too. Rose ended the season as one of the leading scorers in the league.

Rose was proud of his individual achievements. But he was more proud that he had helped the Bulls achieve the best record in the NBA. Rose played so well that he was named the league's Most Valuable Player (MVP)!

The Bulls won their first-round playoff series. Then they won their second-round series. That set up the conference finals against the Miami Heat. The winner would go to the NBA Finals. The Bulls' dream season ended there. The Heat had some great players. They overpowered Rose and the Bulls.

Another reason for the Bulls' improved play was their new coach, Tom Thibodeau. Coach Thibodeau was sometimes hard on Rose. But Rose did not mind. He knew the coach wanted him to be as good as he could be.

After winning the Rookie of the Year and MVP awards, Rose has his sights on the NBA title.

Rose was disappointed. He had hoped to lead Chicago to its first NBA title since 1998. The tough series against the Heat showed Rose just how hard that is. But Rose has proven he knows how to improve. In his first three NBA seasons, he went from the Rookie of Year to an All-Star to the MVP. He led the Bulls to the best record and to the conference finals. The only thing left for Derrick Rose to do is to win an NBA championship.

FUN FACTS AND QUOTES

- During Derrick Rose's senior year of high school, he was named Mr. Basketball in the state of Illinois. That meant he was considered the best high school basketball player in the entire state.

- Rose's agent is B. J. Armstrong. Before he became an agent, Armstrong was a guard for the Chicago Bulls, just like Rose.

- Even the guys Rose plays against love to watch him play. Marvin Williams is a forward for the Atlanta Hawks. But Williams admitted after one game that he was not just a player, he was also a fan of Rose's.

- The public address announcer at Bulls games usually introduces players by saying what college they played for. For his first game with the Bulls, though, Rose asked the announcer to say he was from Chicago even though he went to Memphis. The Bulls fans loved it.

- Rose got a chance to play basketball with President Barack Obama. When they were done playing, Rose joked that he wished the president played for the Bulls.

WEB LINKS

To learn more about Derrick Rose, visit ABDO Publishing Company online at **www.abdopublishing.com**. Web sites about Rose are featured on our Book Links page. These links are routinely monitored and updated to provide the most current information available.

GLOSSARY

assist
A pass that leads directly to a made shot.

crossover
Dribbling the ball from one hand to the other.

draft
In the NBA, an event held each June in which the teams take turns selecting from among the top college and international players.

dunk
To jump high enough to drop the ball instead of shooting it into the hoop.

hype
Having high expectations for a player.

rebound
In basketball, to grab the ball after a missed shot.

recruiters
People who try to convince a player to join their team.

rookie
A first-year player in the NBA.

varsity
The main team that represents a school.

veteran
Someone who has been playing a sport for a long time.

INDEX

FURTHER RESOURCES

Howell, Brian. *Chicago Bulls*, Edina, MN: ABDO Publishing Co., 2012.

Ladewski, Paul. *Megastars*. New York: Scholastic, 2011.

Woog, Adam. *Derrick Rose*. Detroit: Lucent Books, 2010.